Bill Clinton:
Man of the Public

BY

Dr. Charles K. Aka

ISBN: 0-7596-8734-X

This book is printed on acid free paper.

1stBooks - rev. 4/5/02

This book is dedicated to Chelsea Victoria Clinton

iv

Table of Contents

"And they that shall be of thee shall build the old waste places: thou shalt raise up the foundations of many generations; and thou shalt be called, the repairer of the breach, the restorer of paths to dwell in."

(Isaiah 58:12)

FORWORD

The political energy of America has grasped the attention of people from around the world. Immigrants that seek America as their home may find themselves perplexed at America's political culture and the freedom that it renders its citizens. Although the political energy that surrounds this free world may be complicated to understand to those seeking to be free, America is a place where freedom is enjoyed. America's 'Declaration of Independence,' since its inception in 1776, supports this freedom. It is a document that explains the endemic nature of the freedom that the citizens of this country have come to be hopeful towards. Its citizens protect, support and maintain the lifestyle this document represents; by sacrificing their lives and the lives of others that may choose to compromise or end America's freedom, as it is understood. As complicated as our political structure and culture may appear to outsiders, many seek after the dynamics that encompass this free society. Other diverse cultures proclaim our politics and ideals ('America Land of the Free') and settle in America making it their home, just as the author Dr. Charles Aka has done.

Dr. Aka had visited America often over twenty years. It was not until 1993 that he settled in America. Democrat elected President William Jefferson Clinton was in office. Dr. Aka admired President Clinton; he had been following reports of the media and had become overwhelmingly inquisitive with the way the media handled and reported on his personal and political life. Dr. Aka questioned how a great leader, such as the President of the United States could be so disrespected, as if he had no stature, treated as a commoner! Dr. Aka is from Africa, (Ghana), and his understanding of respect and loyalty rendered its leaders, is revered in his native land. He compared the treatment of President Clinton to the treatment of the leaders in Africa and became disillusioned. How can such a great country that strives for so many good things for the betterment of humanity act this way towards its leader? Dr. Aka had decided to do independent research that would support his understanding the truth about President William J. Clinton, whom was being portrayed in the media with a vengeance.

Dr. Aka's political point of view is derived from a strong patriarchal political structure and culture. As he traced President Clinton's career as a politician, his research led him to the adage, 'sex and politics do not mix'. America's political culture and structure today is more inclusive of women who are in more significant political roles and are more sensitive to how women are portrayed and treated in the political arena. Therefore, women who are citizens of this nation play an intricate part in helping to create, organize, maintain, and support America's political agendas. It is within this political framework that the plight of President Clinton unfolded and expanded to a progressive level that settled with impeachment hearings. The American citizens of this great nation in general, have always played a significant role as the country's political conscience and power network. Regardless of your stature in this society or political affiliation, as an American you are allowed to think what you want to think, say what you want to say, whenever you want to say it, how you want to say it, (within the law) and it is considered exercising your freedom.

The beginning of Dr. Aka's research journey may have been to learn the truth about President William J. Clinton, Democrat, husband, father, and about the political reprisals that had been engaged against him. However, what he found was Americans exercising their freedom at its utmost level! The reports presented by his enemies, a large percentage of his political opponents and their constituents in the media were deemed retaliatory, by an overwhelming majority of the American public that expressed adoration, respect, empathy, and sympathy for President Clinton's exposed plight. President William J. Clinton will be remembered as one of the most controversial, and colorful political figures in our time. The majority of the American people freely revered him during his term as president and continues to freely revere him as one of America's great leaders. Author Dr. Charles K. Aka portrays a 'birds eye' view about <u>Bill Clinton: Man of the Public</u>

October 28, 2001

Theresa A.

Chapter One
HISTORICAL BACKGROUND

The world has never seen a President so lucky, so tempted, so disgraced, so sorry, so humorous, so victorious, and so blessed like William Jefferson (Bill) Clinton.

Bill Clinton, the forty-second (42nd) President of the United States of America was born in Hope, Arkansas on the nineteenth of August, 1946. Clinton is an Arkansan and was the fifth generation. His mother's name was Virginia Kelly. She first married a gentleman named William Jefferson Blyth III. He was an automotive equipment salesman. Later, Mr. Blyth was killed in an uncommon automobile accident some months before little Bill Clinton was born. His kind and grateful mother named him William Jefferson Blyth, IV after his late dear father.

When Bill was only four years old, his mother left him with her parents, Hardey and Mattie Hawkins. His widowed, devoted, and courageous mother continued her education and came out successfully as a nurse-anesthesiologist. His grandparents controlled a small store in a "black" dominated neighborhood. His grandparents and his mother seriously taught young Bill

Clinton that, racism and discrimination were purely erroneous, despite the racist practices of the south in the 1950s.

Bill was eight years old when his beloved mother had her second marriage with Mr. Roger Clinton. After their glamorous marriage, the family moved to Hot Springs, Arkansas. It was believed that Roger Clinton's household was an uncomfortable one. Nevertheless, in an indication of family union, the smart and cunning William Jefferson Blyth willfully changed his last name to Clinton at the age of fifteen. His stepfather Roger was always under the influence of alcohol, which resulted in a series of domestic violence incidents. At the tender age of fifteen, he boldly made it clear to his dear alcoholic father that he would sacrifice to defend both his dear mother and half brother Roger Jr. from any further mistreatment and humiliation. That courageous attempt marked the beginning of William Jefferson (Bill) Clinton's humanitarian and leadership qualities.

As an ambitious child, young Clinton thought about many professions. He wanted either to be a musician (saxophonist) or a medical doctor. Despite his hardships during his early years, he excelled in school. He became a student leader and very active.

As a selected member of a delegation of the American Legion Boys' Nation high school, Bill luckily met then President John F. Kennedy. After that historical meeting with President Kennedy, he made up his mind or had an opinion to indulge in active politics.

Bill Clinton started his college education at Georgetown University in 1964. As a social student in a college, he involved himself in a movement against the Vietnam War, likewise to the civil rights struggle. In his hometown Arkansas in 1966, he worked as a summer intern for Arkansas Senator J. William Fulbright, who was at the moment the leader of antiwar sentiment in the U.S.

senate. He was then a student in Washington D.C. when the activist Martin Luther King Jr. was killed.

Bill generously used his car with the assistance of a good friend, delivered food and medical supplies to neighborhoods affected by the disturbed condition that followed Reverend King's assassination.

Young and handsome, Bill Clinton graduated from Georgetown University in 1968 with a B.Sc.in International Affairs. People who knew Bill very well regarded him as a born politician. In other words, a gifted and an active public man. Later

Clinton was awarded a Rhodes scholarship and spent two years as a post-graduate student at Oxford University in Great Britain. It was there in 1969 that he wrote a convincing or inviting letter to an army colonel in Arkansas ROTC program about his draft eligibility and his opposition to the war in Vietnam. In his letter he made it known about his firm position both in terms of the draft and in terms of his later "political potential". It was at this early age that he became more concerned with his electability as a politician.

Bill Clinton became a student at Yale University Law School in 1970. As a first

Dr. Charles K. Aka

year student at Yale, he served as a campaign coordinator for Mr. Joe Duffy, who was an antiwar candidate for the U.S. senate from Connecticut. While still a law student, he again worked with the renowned writer Honorable Taylor Branch as campaign coordinator in Texas for presidential candidate George McGovern.

William Jefferson (Bill) Clinton fortunately met the smart, brilliant and beautiful young lady, Hillary Rodham, at Yale University. She was also a law student.

Immediately after graduation from Yale, Bill and Hillary were given jobs on the staff of the House of Representatives committee that was thinking about the impeachment of a great and very remarkable Republican President Richard Nixon. Bill Clinton decided to return to Arkansas when Hillary later offered a new job or worked as a member of the House staff. He later went into private practice in Fayetteville, the center of Arkansas politics, and also began teaching at the University of Arkansas Law School.

Dr. Charles K. Aka

Chapter Two
POLITICAL WORK IN
ARKANSAS

Bill Clinton first ran for Congress in 1974 against President Richard Nixon's strong supporter John Paul Hammerschmidt. Bill lost the election but it was a very close vote. In a heavily Republican state, running as the incumbent, Hammerschmidt got only fifty one point five percent (51.5%) of the vote.

In the same year that Clinton lost his first election, Hillary Rodham joined Bill Clinton in Fayetteville and also taught at the University of Arkansas Law School. Bill

11

and Hillary happily got married on October 11, 1975. They left Fayetteville for Little Rock when Bill Clinton was elected attorney general of the state of Arkansas, a post he held from1977 to 1979. He became the golden boy of Arkansas politics. Bill ran for the office of Governor of Arkansas in 1978. He was elected and became the youngest governor of any state since Harold E. Stassen was elected in 1938 at the age of thirty one. In his first term in office, Bill Clinton tried to make many changes, and those changes were not entirely popular, including an attempt to raise automobile licensing fees.

Bill and Hillary had a bouncing and pretty daughter who they named Chelsea Victoria on February 27, 1980. That same year in November, Ronald Reagan won a landslide victory against President Jimmy Carter, and Bill Clinton lost his try for reelection as governor of Arkansas to Republican candidate Frank White. After this great loss he realized that some of his policies in the past as a governor contributed to the failure of his reelection.

In 1982, Bill Clinton campaigned vigorously again against Frank White for reelection. He humbly and vividly elucidated to the electorate that he had learned well the mistakes of the past that led to his failure and that he was comfortably elected with fifty-five percent (55 %) of the vote. It was then that he earned his nickname, "the Comeback Kid." Bill actively and successfully served as governor of Arkansas until 1992. In fact, his supporters truly believed him to be an activist. He severely advocated for welfare, school and health reform with combined results. In Democratic national politics, Bill Clinton continued to be more active. In post-segregation southern politics too, Bill developed profound concern as an advocator or a new voice.

In 1988, Clinton distinguished himself at the Democratic Convention when he gave a protracted speech to nominate Massachusetts Governor Michael Dukakis as the party's presidential candidate. Though the speech was not well received, he continued to be active in national politics. His mates voted him as most effective Governor in 1991 and that same year he was selected as chairman of the Democratic Leadership Conference. Other southerners such as Albert Gore of Tennessee worked along with Bill Clinton to shift control of the Democratic Party away from the northeastern liberal wing to form a new party constituency.

Dr. Charles K. Aka

Chapter Three
ELECTION TO THE
PRESIDENCY

Bill Clinton announced in October, 1991 that, he was entering the 1992 race for president. Bill had a lot of competition for the Democratic nomination, and many of those candidates professed to be the option or choice that presented a change from the party's past and a change to defeat the incumbent president, George Bush.

Before the party's primary in 1992 in New Hampshire, he had encountered many hindrances and hardships. Clinton is

17

somebody who emerged from a small state that was considered by many as unskilled and underdeveloped as compared to other states of the United States. Faultfinders sensed or perceived that he had no experience on the federal level and lacked any understanding of foreign policy. In response, Bill declared emphatically that his strengths rest in the fact that he was not linked to a Washington power base and for that reason had a fresh view or vision to bring to government.

Bill Clinton was again troubled or afflicted by charges of personal disgrace that included allegations of sexual links with women apart from his wife and questions concerning his draft status during the Vietnam War. The said events were the genesis of his numerous problems.

He did not lose hope but persevered to stay in the race, patiently seeing things progress until the 1992 Democratic Convention, where he was chosen as his party's presidential candidate to challenge President George Bush. Bill, who also believed in the strength and the effectiveness of the youth in American politics and administration, without any hesitation, selected the young Senator Albert Gore of the state of Tennessee as his running mate.

Bill thought of concentrating his campaign on economic issues, particularly about his understanding of the hardships of the unemployed and underemployed, as well as the universal concern over health care. Bill Clinton was elected president of the United States of America in November 1992, defeating the incumbent Republican George Bush and the rich and third party candidate Honorable Ross Perot. Many times in his campaign, he referred to his birthplace claiming, "I still believe in a place called Hope." This victory made him the luckiest among the American youth that met the late and renowned President John F.

Kennedy about three and half decades before. He was the first President since Franklin Roosevelt who had never served in the armed forces. Bill was also the first Rhodes scholar and the first sitting governor since Franklin Roosevelt to be elected President.

While in office, he directed much of his attention to economic issues as interest rates and unemployment started to fall. Bill Clinton nominated Hillary Rodham Clinton as the head of a task force authorized to examine possibilities for large-scale health care reform. He was able to enact most of his proposals or schemes for the "change"

21

issue that controlled his campaign by the assistance of a Democratic majority in both the House of Representatives and the Senate. Likely the most hard and painstaking of the passed legislation was the 1993 North American Free Trade Agreement (NAFTA) making a single trading block of the United States, Canada and Mexico.

Approaching the end of his first term, a new episode menaced President Clinton's credibility. The incident was named "Whitewater" for the suspicious Arkansas land deals in which both Bill and Hillary Clinton were profoundly involved. This unfortunate episode caused great distress, fatigue and havoc, and almost brought Bill Clinton and his betterhalf Hillary into total disrepute. The same "Whitewater" scandal miserably landed some prominent people into prison in chains including the well-educated and beautiful lady Susan McDougal, for refusing to testify before the federal grand jury in Little Rock, Arkansas. The second attempt to revive or investigate "Whitewater" was completely dismissed by the independent counsel Robert Ray on September 20, 2000. Commenting on this scandal that has hung over the White House for eight good years, Bill said, "it was a sham from the beginning. It was a put-up deal. I think that this whole Whitewater business will be looked upon by any rational observer in history as an absurd episode in American history which didn't amount to a hill of beans."

William Jefferson (Bill) Clinton was re-elected to a second term on November 5, 1996, as the United States President. He incredibly won the election by a landslide, beating one of the American's most gentlemen and respected Bob Dole with forty nine percent (49%) of the popular vote and 379 electoral votes. Bill Clinton continues to campaign for the important issues in which he dearly believes.

Chapter Four
CONSPIRACY AND SCANDAL

Before Paula Jones filed a lawsuit charging that President Bill Clinton sexually harassed her in an Arkansas hotel room in May 1994, he, under great pressure, asked that a special prosecutor be named to investigate his "Whitewater" land dealings in early January 1994. Attorney General Reno selected Robert Fiske to be responsible. Later, after reauthorization of the Independent Counsel Act, a panel of three federal appeals court judges appointed former President George Bush administration Solicitor General Kenneth

Starr to take over Mr. Fiske's investigation in August 1995.

The former state clerk Paula Jones declared that Bill Clinton summoned her to a room in a Little Rock hotel in 1991, dropped his trousers and seriously demanded that she (Jones) should have sex with him when he was a governor of Arkansas. Paula Jones further alleged that because of her harassment she suffered emotional distress. Jones emphatically claimed that, should Bill Clinton deny that allegation, she could describe "distinguishing characteristics" of his genitals, that is to say, there could be a trial focusing on the shape of President Clinton's penis. Mr. Clinton openly denied these charges and once asked a judge who was dealing with Jones' sexual harassment complaint to toss out or stop the case. Judge Susan Webber Wright, a former law student of Bill Clinton who was handling the case, finally dismissed Paula Jones' case.

Paula Jones, who was suing Bill Clinton for sexual harassment, initially sued the Arkansas State Trooper Danny Lee Ferguson and later dropped her suit against Ferguson when Ferguson's lawyer began to research her personal life. Jones also might have taken her shots in a trial simply because a man claimed he picked Paula Jones up in a bar and had sex with her in a parking lot a few months before her alleged encounter with Bill Clinton.

The Paula Jones episode served as bait to attract a chain of women to disclose President Clinton's illicit sexual relationship or approach with them. Their insidious stories received widespread coverage in the media including radio and television. The following is a string of female accusers of Bill Clinton besides Paula Jones.

Gennifer Flowers, a longtime friend of President Bill Clinton, claimed that she had a twelve-year affair with him. Gennifer Flowers is also a lady who allegedly knows most of Bill Clinton's weaknesses, secrets, and his bad sexual habits. According to Bill Clinton, he truly admitted under oath that he consensually had sex with Gennifer Flowers once in 1977. Previously, he had denied Flowers' claim that they had a twelve-year affair.

Kathleen Willey, an ex-White House aide who called herself a "Harassment Victim" confessed that the very day in 1993 when her husband committed suicide, Bill Clinton grabbed her breast and put her hand on his erect penis when she went to talk with him about a full-time job because of family financial troubles.

However, less than a month after this incident, Willey wrote Bill Clinton by saying, "after this bittersweet year, my first resolution for 1994 will be the pursuit of a meaningful job, and hope it will be here." The following note was another, which was written by Kathleen Willey herself and ended with this remark:

Dear Mr. President, what a wonderful week you have had! Congratulations on all your well-deserved successes. I would very much like to have a few minutes of your time to discuss something of importance to me. I will wait to hear from you—Fondly Kathleen.

"Fondly Kathleen" was intentionally said to Bill Clinton, whom she (Willey) said groped her. In all, Willey sent Bill ten good notes after the incident or her charges that Bill Clinton groped her in a private room off the Oval Office.

Cristy Zercher, a former flight attendant of Governor Bill Clinton's 1991-1992 campaign plane. This beautiful young lady claimed that Bill Clinton indiscriminately fondled her in the jet in 1992. Zercher continued that the future President also barraged or attacked her with rude gestures and crude sexual jokes about barnyard animals. She emphatically said that the Democratic presidential candidate once invited her to join him in the campaign jet's bathroom while his pants were unzipped. She seriously quoted Mr. Clinton as telling her, "I could really get lost in those blue eyes." Cristy said that when Bill Clinton first met her and the two other attendants on the jetliner in 1991, his immediate reaction was "Wow, this is great! What'd they do, go out and hire models?" Zercher finally disclosed that, on an overnight flight from

New York to California, Bill Clinton began rubbing her left breast and asking her intimate questions about her two failed marriages while his dear wife Hillary slept a few feet away.

Monica Lewinsky, the former White House intern. She began working as an unpaid intern in the office of the Chief of Staff, Leon Panetta in July 1995. Monica Lewinsky is young, beautiful, well educated, and sexually liberated. After only four months in the White House, she began her relationship or had first sexual encounter with President Bill Clinton. In April 1996, Lewinsky was transferred to the Pentagon after White House aides complained that she was spending too much time in the West Wing. In the relationship between Bill Clinton and Lewinsky, they both gave several gifts to each other to establish and strengthen their secret love. Lewinsky who was then twenty-one, carried a grudge against the selfish people who banished her to the Pentagon from the White House because she was getting too close to the fifty-two year-old President.

Monica Lewinsky thought that her liaison or link did not hurt the work she and President Clinton were doing. It was between them and never was their business to occupy themselves with. This was about a man and a woman, and not a President and an intern.

In Monica Lewinsky's late interview with ABC's Barbara Walters, she had this to say: "I first didn't find President Clinton attractive. With his big red nose and rough or ugly, wiry-looking gray hair, and an old guy." There were tons and tons of women in the White House with crushes on him (Clinton) and I (Monica) thought, "these people are just crazy. They have really bad taste in men." Monica continued, "from the beginning there was a very intense sexual attraction and I did not necessarily think a sexual attraction was an erroneous thing and still do not feel that way. Lewinsky disclosed, "We would talk, we would laugh, we would tell jokes. Bill was very tender with me. He was pretty sweet and affectionate. Monica said she approached President Clinton later and boldly told him she was in love with him, which meant a lot to her. She admitted that Bill Clinton never said he love her, but she added that, "there were times" when she believed he (Bill Clinton) felt that way. "The way especially he looked at me and the way he touched me was terrific. Monica said Clinton's present of Walt Whitman's "Leaves of Grass" is the kind of gift that you would not hold in a certain place in your heart."

Monica Lewinsky further said, during their flirtation, he (Bill) undressed her with his eyes, and both clicked at an incredible level. Monica said, "People have made it seem so demeaning for me but was not, it was very exciting and the irony is that I had the first orgasm of the relationship with Bill Clinton." Lewinsky disclosed that once she and Bill Clinton became romantically involved, they would have long conversations at the White House. "Bill would sit in the rocking chair and I (Monica) would end up sitting on the floor at his feet with my elbows on his knees and would just talk." Monica confessed that Bill Clinton endeavored to reassure her when she complained she was feeling like a sex object or considered cheap. She said, Bill never wanted her to feel bad, alone, and distressed. He frequently admired her figure or form.

Monica Lewinsky described Bill Clinton as "a human being, a regular person, a good kisser, and very sweet." She called Clinton her "sexual soul mate" and said their chemistry clicked from their first kiss. She confessed that Bill did things to make her happy and content during their relationship. Monica said, she secretly met President

Clinton at White House, and also conducted several late-night phone sex conversations with him. Lewinsky again called Clinton "a very sensual man who has a lot of sensual feelings" that conflict with his deep religious beliefs. "I think he tries to hold himself back and then he can't anymore because it is an energy you cannot, can't ignore."

Monica Lewinsky sadly commented on the endlessly replayed snippet of videotape showing her in a black beret hugging the President of the United States of America at an event held on the 6th of November, 1996. Lewinsky said she considered that that day was the real beginning of the end of her clandestine relationship with Bill Clinton. It was because Bill did not call her as she expected after that meeting or encounter. Monica painfully lamented that she was grossly offended about the events of President Clinton and also when he (Clinton) referred to her as "that woman" in his grand jury deposition, after going through the hideous reputation and national humiliation. Hence, Lewinsky bitterly described Bill Clinton as "a much bigger liar than she ever thought and also see him as selfish man who lies all the time."

Monica Lewinsky has painstakingly testified twenty three times under oath about her mischievous eighteen months friendship with President Bill Clinton. She has been seriously under fire by FBI agents, prosecutors, and the U.S. Congress. Monica is considered as "America's most famous ex-intern."

Linda Tripp, an employee of the Pentagon who comfortably makes about ninety two thousand dollars ($92,000) a year. Tripp induced her young friend Monica Lewinsky into a trap to incriminate President Bill Clinton or to bring him to justice. Tripp secretly and maliciously taped twenty hours conversation with Monica and also intentionally handed over the tapes to the office of independent counsel Kenneth Starr which caused the "sexgate scandal" that resulted in the attempt to oust Bill Clinton from office. Linda Tripp betrayed Lewinsky because she hated the White House or had a false idea about the Clintons. At one point, she (Tripp) claimed that Hillary Clinton was jealous of her because she (Hillary) suspected that she (Tripp) was having an affair with President Bill Clinton.

The forty-nine year old Maryland mother of two children remained unrepentant of her betrayal of Lewinsky's confidence. She proudly confessed that New York literary agent, Lucianne Goldberg, dragged her into the scandal. She confidently said, "it never occurred to me to go to independent counsel Kenneth Starr." Linda Tripp said that a long time Bill Clinton enemy Goldberg pushed her to expose Monica Lewinsky's confessions and secretly recorded their girl-talk phone calls. She alleged that, it was Lucianne Goldberg who went to Kenneth Starr and Paula Jones' lawyers. Goldberg did not deny Tripp's accusation.

Monica Lewinsky and her family called the "Sexgate" taper Linda Tripp as a meddlesome witch, a praying mantis and a delusional brainwasher. They also described Tripp as a disgruntled, manipulative woman of the century. Lewinsky personally compared Linda Tripp to Svengali, a character in a 19th century novel who, through hypnosis, transformed a talentless young woman into a famous vocalist. Lewinsky thought she was trusting in a friend when she poured out the story of her affair with the President. Instead, she was being invited or attracted into a big trap, the unwitting bait with which to apprehend William Jefferson (Bill) Clinton.

There were two major factors, which brought about the wicked conspiracy and the sex scandal of Bill Clinton. The first factor was the diabolic plan to disgrace and pull him down by the enemies or opponents immediately after Bill Clinton's election as the President of the United States of America in 1992, when they genuinely and evidently saw his unchallenged and effective leadership that would perpetuate the Democratic Party leadership in the nation. The second factor was the Paula Jones sexual harassment case against him (Bill Clinton), which was influenced or engineered by his long-time enemy Lucianne Goldberg, a literary agent of New York in 1994. This Paula Jones matter also served as the immediate cause of Bill Clinton's dilemma. Hence, the Supreme Court ruled on May 27, 1997 that Paula

Jones could pursue her lawsuit while he (President Clinton) was in office, which his lawyers initially and strongly tried to argue against.

As a result of Linda Tripp and Lucianne Goldberg's clandestine and wicked plan against young Monica Lewinsky for making her taped conversations about her sexual relationship with Bill Clinton to both the office of independent counsel Kenneth Starr and Paula Jones lawyers, the former White House intern Monica Lewinsky's name was included in a list of potential witnesses in Jones' lawsuit in December, 1997. Lewinsky was later served with subpoena to appear at a deposition for the Paula Jones suit and to turn over the mentioned gifts from President Bill Clinton. In January 1998, Monica Lewinsky signed an affidavit for Paula Jones' case and declared that she had no sexual relationship with President Bill Clinton as alleged. This infuriated Linda Tripp, who was strongly supported by Lucianne Goldberg to provide Starr's office with taped conversations between herself and Monica Lewinsky.

Dr. Charles K. Aka

Chapter Five
KENNETH STARR SEX SCANDAL INVESTIGATION

In the middle part of January 1998, a court panel gave Kenneth Starr authority to investigate Monica Lewinsky matters. Before Kenneth Starr was given the authority to investigate President Clinton's elicit sexual activities, some important dignitaries from both advanced and the third world countries humbly and respectfully advised the U.S. Senate to generously forgive their young, smart, humanitarian, and industrious President Bill Clinton of any wrongdoing, and endeavored to focus on other important matters or issues. Amongst them were the President of Mexico, Ernesto Zedillo, British Prime Minister Tony Blair, Ehud Barak who was then the leader of the opposition Labor Party in Israel, former Prime Minister of Israel Benjamin Netanyahu, Yasser Arafat of Palestine, former President Jimmy Carter, George Bush, King Hussein of Jordan and President Nelson Mandela of South Africa. Others included Reverend Billy Graham, Pope John Paul II, Jesse Jackson, Al Sharpton, Arch-Bishop Desmond Tutu just to mention a few. Again, the majority of about 73% of the American population voted against any investigation or impeachment trial of

President Clinton. Yet, all the noble advice fell onto deaf ears. In other words, the humble appeals made by many people in respect of Bill Clinton's investigation and impeachment proved futile in defense of the rule of law as claimed by his opponents but to the detriment of the American masses and the views of the outside world.

In fact, after the revealed tapes by Linda Tripp, some prosecutors tried several occasions to confront Monica Lewinsky and they were unsuccessful to seek her cooperation to incriminate herself and the President of the United States. Immediately after Lewinsky's testimony, Kenneth Starr's counsel summoned President Bill Clinton to also testify in Jones' lawsuit against him and he categorically denied a sexual relationship with Lewinsky. In President Clinton's deposition in January 1998, he declared, "I did not have sexual relations with that woman…I never told anybody to lie."

In March 1998, a former President Clinton aide Kathleen Willey appeared on CBS' "60 Minutes" and said that Bill Clinton groped her in the White House when she went to talk with President Clinton about a full-time job in 1993. Exactly two weeks after Willey's accusation, U.S. District Judge Susan Webber Wright in

Arkansas dismissed Paula Jones' lawsuit against Bill Clinton.

Under immunity from prosecution, Monica Lewinsky testified before Kenneth Starr's grand jury and President Clinton also underwent more than four hours of questioning before the same grand jury on April 6th and 17th, 1998. In Bill Clinton's televised speech, he then said, "I did have a relationship with Monica Lewinsky that was not appropriate. It constituted a critical lapse in judgment and personal failure on my part for which I am solely and completely responsible."

On September 9, 1998, Kenneth Starr told House leaders that he found "substantial and credible information that might constitute grounds for impeachment." Ken Starr delivered thirty-six (36) boxes holding two copies of his detailed report and the supporting evidence that very day.

The thirty-six boxes comprised fifty thousand (50,000) pages of grand jury testimony, which were comfortably conveyed by special vehicle and security men to the doorstep of the House of Representatives. There were four hundred and forty five (445) pages in Ken Starr's referral to the House. There were sixty-seven (67) people who testified before the Starr grand jury. The cost of the Clinton investigation by Ken Starr was a huge sum of fifty-eight million U.S. dollars ($58,000,000).

In fact, the strong decision or ruling by Kenneth Starr that President Clinton should be impeached because of adverse findings about him, the unsympathetic and very arrogant way he (Kenneth Starr) presented his boxes of prejudicial report to Congress, Ken Starr and his team of prosecutors intimidation of Monica Lewinsky and her beloved Marcia Lewis during their interrogation, the open support of House prosecutors or managers just to say a few, made the majority of the American citizens of conscience believed that he (Ken Starr) was one of Bill Clinton's conspirators and severe enemy.

Chapter Six
HOUSE IMPEACHMENT INQUIRY

On October 5, 1998, by a twenty one (21) to sixteen (16) party line vote, the House Judiciary Committee opened a formal investigation into grounds for impeachment. Also, on the 8th of October, 1998, the House voted two hundred and fifty-eight (258) to one hundred and seventy-six (176) to authorize or hold an impeachment inquiry about President Bill Clinton's sexual immorality. Though Republicans retained control of Congress, the House Democrats successfully picked up five House seats in the election held on November 3, 1998. The national polls conducted also showed that two-thirds (2/3) of the American voters did not want President Bill Clinton to be impeached.

In another development on November 13, 1998, both the lawyers for Bill Clinton and Paula Jones finally agreed that, a sum of eight hundred and fifty thousand U.S. dollars ($850,000) be paid to Paula Jones as a settlement to drop her sexual-harassment lawsuit, with no apology from him (Clinton) or admission of guilt. In the same week, Ken Starr announced that President Clinton was off the hook or had no adverse findings against him in two of his probes, the 1993 White House Travel Office firings and the procurement of FBI files on Republicans by White House operatives. Kenneth Starr's ethics adviser, Sam Dash, resigned to strongly demonstrate his objection to Starr's testimony before House Judiciary Committee in support of Clinton's impeachment.

In November 27, 1998, House Judiciary Chairman, Henry J. Hyde, asked President Bill Clinton to admit or deny eighty-one (81) findings from the Ken Starr report. Answering questions from Chairman Henry Hyde, Bill Clinton wrote to the Judiciary

Committee that the testimony he gave in the Monica Lewinsky affair was not false and misleading as the Committee considered. White House presented its defense. Both Republican and Democratic lawyers went before the House Judiciary Committee to make their final arguments. Along party line votes, the Committee approved four articles of impeachment and rejected a Democratic resolution on censure. The impeachment debate began in the House.

After one week that President Clinton responded to the House Judiciary Committee's eighty one (81) questions, the Committee approved impeachment articles

1, 2 and 3, which accused Bill Clinton, the President of the United States of perjury in the Paula Jones deposition and in his grand jury testimony, and of obstruction of justice in the Jones case. The committee also approved a fourth and final article, including charges of perjury regarding Bill Clinton's responses to its questions. The Committee rejected a substitute resolution backed by Democrats that instead would censure Bill Clinton for reprehensible conduct. Coincidentally, the launching of U.S. military strikes against Iraq on December 17, 1998 delayed the debate on articles of impeachment.

Dr. Charles K. Aka

Chapter Seven
BILL CLINTON IMPEACHED

The second presidential impeachment trial in the U.S. history started on December 19, 1998 in the Senate. The House impeached President William Jefferson (Bill) Clinton on two articles. The first, charging that he committed perjury in his August 17th grand jury testimony, passed two hundred and twenty eight (228) to two hundred and six (206). A second charging obstruction of justice passed two hundred and twenty one (221) to two hundred and twelve (212). Charges of perjury in the Paula Jones deposition and abuse of power failed to pass. The day after Bill Clinton was impeached, polls showed his approval rating continue to rise, hitting nearly seventy three percent (73%) in some serious surveys.

On January 7, 1999, the Senate opened the impeachment trial of Bill Clinton, the youngest and forty-second (42nd) President of the United States of America. Chief Justice William Rehnquist presided over the historic five week impeachment trial. The next day, January 8, 1999, the Senate unanimously approved a plan for the impeachment trial, but deferred decision on whether to call witnesses. From January 14-16, 1999, the House managers presented their case to the Senate. Between January 19th and 21st, 1999, the White House also presented its defense. On the 22nd and 23rd, Senators questioned both House managers and White House lawyers. Under the order of the trial judge, House prosecutors privately questioned Monica Lewinsky on January 24, 1999 about her affair with President Bill Clinton.

After two good weeks of heated arguments which was the 27 of February, 1999 by House prosecutors and Bill Clinton's lawyers, only one democrat broke ranks and the Senate voted fifty six (56) to forty four (44) against dismissal of charges.

By the same vote, the Senate agreed to authorize subpoenas for questioning of Monica Lewinsky, presidential pal Vernon Jordan and White House aide Sidney Blumenthal. The Senate also approved a Republican plan that provided for video-taped depositions. From February 1st through 3rd, 1999, the House managers interviewed Vernon Jordan and Sidney Blumenthal and their deposition video-taped. On February 4th, by a seventy (70) to thirty (30) vote, the Senate rejected calling Lewinsky to testify on the Senate floor. Also by a sixty two (62) to thirty-eight (38) vote, the Senate allowed excerpts from video-taped depositions to be used in presentations to the Senate.

On February 6, 1999, the Senate watched taped testimony from Lewinsky, Jordan and Blementhal as part of final Senate presentations. In other words, the House managers and White House lawyers used segments of taped deposition to buttress or support their cases. On February 8, 1999, the House managers and very experienced and eloquent White House lawyer Charles Ruff made closing arguments to the Senate. The following day, the Senate voted to hold a debate behind closed doors and the session began. The deadlock or disagreement between the members of the two parties in the House was that the Republicans claimed that President Bill Clinton was guilty of perjury and obstruction of justice, which is a serious national crime to remove him from office. The Democrats argued strongly that the charges brought against him (Clinton) represented low crimes that did not warrant his removal from office.

Chapter Eight
BILL CLINTON ACQUITTED

The most remarkable and historical trial of the century after O.J. Simpson's murder trial in 1994 was the presidential impeachment trial of President Bill Clinton of the United States. The trial was the second presidential impeachment trial in U.S. history. The first was the trial against President Andrew Johnson in 1869. Bill Clinton is not the first U.S. president who has been caught up in such a sexual misconduct or an inelegant spectacle. Yes, other past presidents have faced scandals but never in quite this fashion, with talk of

69

presidential private parts and it's treatment in the U.S. Supreme Court.

The trial judge of the century was Chief Justice William H. Rehnquist. He presided over the impeachment trial of President Bill Clinton on February 12, 1999. On this very day, the United States Senate finally assembled to cast the most important votes in their lives to either spare or remove President Bill Clinton from office. The Senate voted on two paramount articles. The first article was perjury and the second was obstruction of justice.

Article one stated as follows, President Clinton "willfully provided perjurious, false and misleading testimony" to independent counsel Kenneth Starr's grand jury concerning, "the details of his relationship" with a government employee, Monica Lewinsky, fed false statements to his lawyer to be repeated before a grand jury, and corruptly tried to "influence the testimony of witnesses and to impede the discovery of evidence" in a civil rights action.

The second article stated that President Clinton "prevented, obstructed, and impeded the administration of justice and has, to that end, engaged personally and through his subordinates and agents in a course of conduct or scheme designed to delay, impede, cover up and conceal the existence of evidence and testimony related to a federal civil rights action brought against him in a duly instituted judicial proceeding."

When the cameras started rolling and "History" throw it's gaze to the Senate floor, the hundred Senators turned serious in the silent chamber. Spectators lined up outside the Capital at 6:30 a.m., matched from down the 30 public seats in the gallery. The articles charging President Clinton with perjury and obstruction of justice were read one last time to the Senate members assembled and the Trial Judge Chief Justice William Rehnquist boomed, "Senators, how say you? Is the respondent William Jefferson Clinton guilty or not guilty?"

One by one as their names were called, senators rose to their feet behind their desks and called out their votes in one hundred and thirty years. In a calm or quiet chamber at 12:36 p.m., Chief Justice William Rehnquist formally declared Bill Clinton was in the clear, that his lies and evasions on the Monica Lewinsky sex scandal cover up would not cost him the White House. "It is therefore ordered and adjudged that...William Jefferson Clinton...acquitted of the charges in the said articles," Justice William Rehnquist announced in the silent chamber.

After thirteen months of scandal and thirty-seven days of trial to end President Clinton's impeachment case, it took only thirty-two minutes interval of solemnity to complete the two anticlimactic votes. The Senate sincerely and respectfully declared President Bill Clinton "not guilty" of perjury by a 55 to 45 vote and acquitted of obstruction of justice by aptly muddled 50-50-well short of two-thirds majority, or 67 votes, required to remove him (Clinton) from office.

After the voting, they applauded one
another and gave Chief Justice William H.
Rehnquist a magnificent plague and a
standing ovation for his honesty and great
achievement in the historic presidential trial
of Bill Clinton. The following was the
statement to Chief Justice Rehnquist read by
the majority Leader Senator Trent Lott:

Now, Mr. Chief Justice on behalf of
myself and the entire United States
Senate, we want to offer you our
thanks and the gratitude of the
American people for your service to
the nation and, throughout this

impeachment court, to this institution."
As our presiding officer during most of
the last five weeks, you have brought
to our proceedings a gentle dignity and
unfailing sense of purpose and
sometimes a sense of humor. By
placing duty above personal
convenience and many other
considerations, you have taught a
lesson in leadership. Your presence in
the chair, the president of the Senate,
following the directives of our
constitution, gave comity to this
chamber and assurance to the nation. I
would like to close with our traditional
Mississippi parting: Y'all come back

soon. But I hope that's not taken the wrong way and not for an occasion like this one. So instead, as you return to your work on the court, in the great marble temple of the law right across the lawn from this Capitol, we salute you, Sir, with renewed appreciation and esteem for a good friend and good neighbor. And now, Mr. Chief Justice, if the Democratic leader will join you, we have a small token of our appreciation. We have a tradition in the Senate that after you have presided over the Senate for 100 hours; we present you with the Golden Gavel Award. And I'm not sure it quite reached a hundred hours, but it's close enough.

Justice Rehnquist reciprocated the gesture by asking permission to thank the senators. With a musty little joke that nonetheless drew gales of laughter, the Chief Justice said, "without objection, I trust." The only surprise about the verdict was the weakness of the support for conviction.

Immediately after his acquittal by the Senate, President Clinton walked to a microphone in the Rose Garden and played his concluding scene as a model of conciliation in a brief statement of apology. He humbly and softly declared:

Now that the Senate has fulfilled it's constitutional responsibility, I want to say again to the American people how profoundly sorry I am for what I said and did to trigger these events and the great burden they have imposed on the Congress and the American people. I also am humbled and very grateful for the support and the prayers I have received from millions of Americans over this past year. Now I ask all Americans, and I hope all Americans here in Washington and throughout our land will rededicate ourselves to the work of serving our nation and building our future together. This can be and this must be a time of reconciliation and renewal for America. Thank you very much.

As the jubilant Bill Clinton moved to leave the Rose Garden after his short and sentimental speech, a cunning reporter asked whether it was time to forgive and forget, Bill Clinton stopped in his tracks, paused, and turned again to the cameras and with a bittersweet smile said, "I believe any person who asks for forgiveness has to be prepared to give it."

Shortly after those votes, a resolution to possibly censure President Clinton for his conduct in the Lewinsky affair died, when it fell short of the two-thirds majority needed to suspend the rules and permit consideration of the measure.

The Senate acquittal of President Bill Clinton was not a victory to boast about or gloat over. The Senate did the right thing to bring relief to both Clinton and the American people. Constitutionally, Bill Clinton was cleansed and the dark cloud over both the White House and the entire American people blew away.

Dr. Charles K. Aka

Chapter Nine
THE EFFECTS OF THE SCANDAL

The general view after the disgrace is that President Clinton damaged the presidency as a result of his misconduct, Congress shamefully suffered from its display of excessive partisanship, and the news media's reputation was severely hurt by its quick appetite for scandal.

In fact, Bill Clinton's conduct, Congress and the news media during the scandal were been clarified. People thought Bill should not be believed, the Congress should not be trusted, and the information from the media needed to be scrutinized. They believed that Clinton was a man of reckless abandon and poor judgment. He (Clinton) put at risk his own position and, more important, destroyed the hopes and hard work of the thousands who had labored for him on the campaign and in his administration. Hence, he is described as a man of situational ethics or morals, who repeatedly puts his own interests ahead of principle. People also believed that Bill Clinton lost the difference between public and private life.

It is true that a president of a country ought to be assessed or evaluated primary on his public actions and speech. But the sexgate of Monica Lewinsky did give a picture or view of the man in full. Enemies and an overly zealous and biased prosecutor put President Clinton in a difficult position. Realizing for the first time the prosecutor's enormous power, the general public was offended by the overreaching Kenneth Starr investigation. Starr was not checked and has miserably and indelibly established troublesome legal precedents. Talking about the stained underwear, private part and cigar was not a celebrity culture in which President Bill Clinton and his entire family were and are content or comfortable with.

At the center of this national quagmire is Bill Clinton, who over six good years became the most popular figure not only in American politics but also in American culture. Because of this unfortunate situation, the whole American nation was forced to live in Bill Clinton's universe. So far as both the senators of the Democrats and some Republicans accepted that, he was not guilty of high crimes and misdemeanors but only guilty of low crimes, people can stand or argue that he lied his way out. What I hope we can all agree with is that sex and politics do not mix.

Concerning Congress, the American public gained a correct view of them. Some were preoccupied at the thought of beating or repeatedly punishing a political enemy. The opponents of Clinton were not able to present a compelling case. They replaced the politics of scandal for the politics of policy or conduct. His enemies both in the Congress and outside joyfully chased or hunted Bill Clinton on his front, after failing to nail him in other severe partisan investigations. Some hypocritically cried self-righteously about honesty and integrity in the government, as they stood behind co-workers with their own character problems. They chose to use the scandal as a political weapon rather than to investigate the matter very critically.

After all this, the American public saw the congressional members for what they truly are. They erroneously ignored public sentiment and fruitful advice. They grossly refused to listen to the collective voice of the great "Melting Pot". Most American citizens preferred that Washington discuss Social Security, Health Care, Education Reforms, Unemployment and so forth rather than semen-stained dresses and cigars.

About the media, the mess caused was hard to measure. The sex scandal of Bill

Clinton arrived and profoundly assisted the media world to expand and become rich. Prognostically, this led to more errors and more sensationalism or deep excitement. It permitted also for wide circulation of information that mainstream news organizations decided was not worthy of publication or airing. The sorry saga did at least appear to sensitize everyday people to ask about society's loss of privacy.

Though these events that went on would have been under way, but maybe less intensely if Monica Lewinsky had never appeared on the national stage or platform. Excuse me to voice that everything was pretty ugly and dirty to experience. No one behaved properly. Perhaps, the American masses would put all these lessons into good use as they watch President Clinton, Congress, and the Press or Media handled the more worldly matters of Washington. It is now time for the two political parties to respect genuinely each other and make peace to the betterment of the entire American people.

There is no doubt that, Bill Clinton's amazing encounter has encouraged him to learn much about the fundamental significance of character and integrity. It has also assisted him to strongly rebuild his family life, the support of both the people he worked with and the majority of the American citizens. His entire life is been rebuilt from the awful mistakes he made. Clinton feels now much more at peace and comfortable than he used to. He has proved that he sincerely needs the sympathy of all.

If today, the scandal did not destroy Bill Clinton but brought him to be outstanding or a different place, the credit goes to the bone of his bones and the flesh of his flesh Hillary and beloved daughter Chelsea. Hillary's reactions to her husband in the time of his darkest predicament supported and encouraged him to stand against all odds and to humiliate his detractors. Her altruism lends itself to a calm echo of common truth to the adage, that behind every great man there is a great, faithful, and strong woman. There is no atom of lie, in that; a helpful wife is a jewel to her husband.

Bill Clinton's daughter Chelsea showed the same integrity, dignity, and strength as her mother. Although Chelsea lived a life of privilege, she never displayed behavior that would embarrass her parents publicly. During the height of the sex scandal, which was publicly waged against her father, and broadcasted around the world, she reacted to her family's humiliation with a show of strong support for her father. Anytime the media portrayed Chelsea, she displayed an impressive image of restraint and was seen smiling, as if to say, this is my father whom I love very dearly, he will always be a great man in my eyes. It is speculated, that it was the energy of their only daughter that helped hold the Clinton's relationship together. The public admired this united family front and identified with it. They supported Bill Clinton overwhelmingly and this too gave him strength to prevail against all odds. Chelsea continued her education and enjoyed her life of privilege, despite the reprisals formed against her father. I think the media understood that the public would not appreciate any undue attack on the wife or the daughter of Bill Clinton.

Chapter Ten

HOW PEOPLE GENERALLY SEE BILL CLINTON

When we honestly look at the entire character of President William Jefferson (Bill) Clinton, he appears to be a man of peace, patience, compassion, understanding, respect, courage and good humor.

People have resentfully found that Bill Clinton lacks integrity because of his past misdeeds, however, he is also found to be very repentant, god-fearing, and a good man. Despite Bill Clinton's shortcomings and his failures particularly to be more honest to his beloved wife Hillary (including his past concubines), he has genuinely proved himself, as a good administrator and a great president heaven and earth know. Apart from being an activist and statesman he is a good family man.

As human, he is prone to sin because no man on our planet earth is perfect. This reminds me of an old adage which says, "to err is human." Now, if Bill Clinton is considered as a liar and unreliable, I suggest the cause may due to the untimely death of his biological father before his birth, and the abusive behavior of his immediate family as alleged including his late stepfather Roger

Clinton. Also Bill's destiny may be the contributing factor or the cause of his dilemma. Yet, the most interesting thing about him (Clinton) is that, after every weakness and failure in his life, he always endeavors to emerge more victorious and strong to shame his adversaries. This also makes him as a man of enormous hope, courage and blessings, especially during his difficult and protracted administration as both governor and president. There is no doubt that the name of Bill Clinton's birthplace, "Hope", has great effect or influence on his entire life.

In the middle of adversity, we again see Bill Clinton as a person full of humility, repentance and profound faith. He boldly, humbly, and respectfully invited the men of God and people of all different faith to the Capitol Hill in time of trouble and also every "prayer Breakfast" to both advise and offer him prayer for forgiveness, repentance, strength, courage, abundant faith and trust in the Lord to firmly stand the test and to overcome his shortcomings and failures. That behavior displayed by Bill Clinton was and is laudable because it is uncommon among rulers of the world. During the crises, which nearly toppled him, he intensively and successfully executed his daily duties and never ceased to attend church services regularly with his dear and supporting family to seek direction, wisdom and refuge in the Lord God.

William Jefferson (Bill) Clinton is ready to forgive with a smile and good heart when grossly offended by both his lovers and enemies. He never let both his personal and legal woes distract him from his White House duties. Bill always has the heart and determination to win the tough battles ahead. Posterity will cherish and profit from his love, generosity, faith, courage, hope, charisma, wisdom, knowledge, determination, eloquence and good humor.

Dr. Charles K. Aka

One of Bill Clinton's aims and policies is that he advocates and also fights for good living, education, health care, and security for all especially the poor and the most vulnerable in the society. Much of his address he expressed concern for the racial division that has plagued America in particular. In his foreign policy too, he strived very vigorously for the "third world or poor countries" of the world to be completely free from debt, poverty, and diseases, which his opponents severely oppose. He honestly tried hard in his administration or leadership to influence the nations of the world to respect and live in total harmony and peace with one another. His peers describe Bill as a man with the heart of a dove. Clinton will only be forced to go to war after all attempts have completely failed and see situations becoming worse or deteriorating. This again portrays him as a man of principle and in favor of freedom and justice.

In a nutshell, Bill Clinton escaped being destroyed by his enemies, and fearlessly returned to fight the more difficult ones within himself. It takes also a good, selfless, energetic, and industrious President to build the economy of a great country. In terms of building the strong economy, achieving unity and peace for America, Bill Clinton has become the true successor of President Franklin Delano Roosevelt who became famous and the loving father of the American nation. He is the world leader who had the dream for the 21st century.

He remains the youngest American President elected since the renowned and humanitarian John F. Kennedy in 1960. Clinton has led the American people to move the country toward balancing the federal budget and lowering the national debt. This progress did occur simply because "There is nothing wrong with America that cannot be cured by what is right with America." With determination, dedication, commitment, hardwork, understanding, patience, and love, Bill's successes have been enormously and awfully increased in the latter part of his administration. He honestly deserves the credit for eight years of economic prosperity because America's success was not a matter of chance, but it was a matter of choice. Clinton's undisputed legacy still remains. He is Moses who has brought Americans to the promise land.

Scandal or no scandal, impeachment or no impeachment, the man of the public, William Jefferson (Bill) Clinton, has successfully finished his second term of office as one of America's dynamic, industrious, intelligent, charismatic, and famous President. Let's sincerely wish him a long life.

Bill Clinton and his beloved family after his effective and successful Presidency chose to live in an historical town called Chappaqua, in New York City. His business office is in Harlem, New York. Some may say that he chose Harlem to mark his name or appellation as "The Black President" of the great America. Many of his political friends and fiends have laughed about his intimate rapport with minorities. But what they don't know that Clinton may never forget, are the people that believed enough in him, elected him as their President, and they prayed for him and prayed with him during his darkest moments. May you continue to be blessed, Mr. Clinton.

ABOUT THE AUTHOR

Dr. Charles K. Aka has learned the standards of the American culture from his many visits from Africa. His desire to make America his new home was pursued in 1993 during the term of President William Jefferson Clinton. Today, Dr. Aka continues to enjoy the freedom that America has to offer. His understanding of America's political culture has increased and he is more familiar with America's political structure. He watches the evening news and reads American newspapers. His concern about America is shown whenever he engages himself in a variety of inquisitive conversations that concern America's power and her enemies. Dr. Aka is becoming an American!

Dr. Aka was born in Ghana, West Africa, and although he misses his native homeland, he feels that he was destined to pursue his dreams in America. He attended Teachers Training College for four years and later earned a doctorate degree in religion. He has been ministering for over thirty years and has presided as a Pastor over the Evangelical Church of Christ, which is a spiritual movement in West Africa; he was the national President in Africa, for the Restored Church of Jesus Christ, and the Church of God of Prophecy. His many affiliations and active leadership has earned him the experience to author such books as; Who Are The True Children and the Church of God; Choosing God or Satan's Standards on Earth; Back to the Early Church; The Motherland of Humanity: A Handbook of Africa, and Black and Colored Religious Women of the Bible. Pastor Oscar Molina presently employs Dr. Aka as a minister. He and his late wife Salomey Korkor Aka's union was blessed with nine children: Dominic, Daniel, Ellen, Janet, Paul, Blaise, Isaac, Delilah, and Diana. The family lives in New York City.

Lightning Source UK Ltd.
Milton Keynes UK
UKHW010649270521
384470UK00001B/70

9 780759 687349